Days like these.

**“A coach is someone who tells you what you don’t want to hear, who have you see what you don’t want to see, so you can be who you have always known you could be.” “You**

**fail all the time, but you aren't a failure until you start blaming someone else." "Do you know what my favorite part of the game is?**

**Don't give up. ...**

**It's not whether you get knocked down; it's whether you get up. ...**

**The interesting thing about coaching is that you have to trouble the comfortable, and comfort the troubled. ...**

**Failures are expected by losers, and ignored by winners.**

# KASHMIR*S FIRST FEMALE FOOTBALL COACH

## INSPIRING STORY OF NADIYA NIGHAT

IMRAN KASHMIRI

Made with ♥ on the Notion Press Platform
www.notionpress.com

J&K

Kashmir*s First Female Football Coach

**A champion is afraid of losing. Everyone else is afraid of winning.**

The key is not the will to win. Everybody has that. It is the will to prepare to win that is important

Victory is in having done your best. If you've done your best, you've won

**The way to get started is to quit talking and begin doing. - ...**

**Your time is limited, so don't waste it living someone else's life. ...**

**The greatest glory in living lies not in falling, but in rising every time we fall. - ...**

**If life were predictable it would cease to be life, and be without flavor. -**

# Contents

# Foreword

***All out, all game, all season." "Put your game face on." "Football is life." "Counting down the days until the Super Bowl.Many people look at me and think they know me but they don't at all.***

Nadiya Nighat hails from the Ram Bagh area of the Srinagar district and is the first female football coach from the Valley who aspires to become the national coach of India. Nadiya has done her schooling at Government High School Natipora, Srinagar and she pursued her higher secondary schooling in Uttarakhand, a state in northern India in the year 2015. In the year 2007, when Nadiya Nighat was 11 years old she went along with some of her friends to Amar Singh College, where she saw some sportsmen practicing football and at that moment she developed a great interest in football. Being in a conservative society, I grew up in the company of my neighborhood children, of which the majority are male," Nadiya shares. When she failed to find the same enthusiasm for the sport among girls, she turned to play with the boys. At 10, Nadiya enrolled herself in Amar Singh College Academy for football coaching. She was the only girl among 47 boys. All the girl students from my locality were least interested in any sport. So, I turned to the boys who always talked football. At times they would discuss the matches they witnessed in Bakshi Stadium which is less than 1km from my home. That day she played her first game there which gave a push to her limits in pursuing a career in this game. I heard them talking and they would forget their studies and regular calls from their parents. I got closer and closer to the game and started accompanying them to practice and friendly matches and at times joined them as a

Goal Keeper.

JAMMU AND KASHMIR

**I felt proud when I discussed football with my teammates. I felt joy in discussing the games when I served as a Goal Keeper**

In our neighborhood there is a retired football coach of the Unity of Kashmir, he saw me playing. Later, he called me and suggested that I collect interested girls in my neighborhood and schoolmates from the nearby locality to form a team. I was very young when I started playing, so no one took it seriously and did not object. Yes, it did invite criticism as we remained busy with football. People talked when we played matches and mixed with boys.

After 6-7 months, I did realize that I was performing well compared to other girls. My coach also took a special interest, in me and I jumped up at the idea of repeating his lessons, and demonstrations to other girls when he was not present.

I started with 5-6 students and it grew up to more than 18-20. I have represented the state in U-15, U-16, and Senior during my last 2-year tenure. The coach took extra care in my routine as I was training to repeat his lessons to others. I made it a point to carry out proper and effective warm-ups and also my exercise.

Being the first Kashmiri female football player and coach.

I cannot put the extra load on my colleagues or trainees as they try to skip it. I explain to them that it is harmful. I have to extract it from them by making them play football-related exercises.

In our state, we need more infrastructure for football. 70% of footballers from the state are poor and 28% belong to the middle class.

Due to the topography of our state, we can play for only 7 months a year. We need all-weather surfaces for playing, and that starts from futsal to full field for football. Establishing a sports school for boys and girls is very necessary. Football is the most liked sport in J&K and we look after it from all angles.

I feel happy to be recognized as a Football coach or player of J&K. It makes me proud and honored at the same time I want to climb up this ladder and achieve the highest levels in Football for the country.

It has to be when the boys from my club, whom I raised as players and also are from my locality and neighborhood, earned the Runners Up Position in their first competition. Encouragement both financially and in the shape of facilities is key. By providing facilities in the shape of infrastructure sports material Good and Sufficient Coaches exposure to see and play against and with senior and players.

**Teamwork makes the dream work.**

Nadiya Nighat:-

In 2010, Nadiya moved to Jammu for participating in 19 School National which was held in the Jammu division. In 2014, she pursued a grass root course with the All India Football Federation. During that course, she learned how to train 6-12 age groups sportspersons. In the year 2015, she got an AFCD license and in the same year, she took part in Playing Senior National which was held at Sharda University, Uttar Pradesh. Nadiya played in Indian Women League (IWL) at Kolhapur in the year 2016 and the same year, she was represented as Sub Junior National Coach in Manipur. In 2017, Nadiya pursued a course tailored for referees through Jammu and Kashmir Football Association in Srinagar, and in the year 2018, she represented Jammu and Kashmir in the 23rd Senior National which was held at Orissa. In the same year, Nadiya night qualify AFC C License and got a job in Mumbai. In the same year 2018, Nadiya started to work as head Coach for the Football Leaders Academy of the under-13 boys youth I league for one year. She also worked as Head Coach in the Alakpura football club in Haryana for girls. Since 2018 she is captain of the Jammu and Kashmir Womens Team. In 2021 she represent senior women's national champions at Kerala. In the same year, she got selected for the Kerala club. Namely Donbosco fc. She played against gokulam team. In 2021 Nadiya join as a Head coach of GOLAZO FC In Pune. she is working for this club. And also nadiya and her team started the residential academy in Pune for boys and girls. Nadiya is not only a coach. She is also a professional footballer.

Hero Junior (U-17) Women*s National Football Championship 2022-23Organized By: AIFF

Later on, she joined lone star Kashmir FC as head coach for the women's wing and as an assistant coach for senior boys in the second division I league. In 2020 Nadiya did ITSO Scouting Level I Course after which she joined Real Kashmir FC as Head coach for women. In 2021, she has been selected for Karnataka State League and in the same year she joined Lone star FC as head coach for the women's wing and assistant coach for senior boys. Females lack support to take up sports because of backwardness and illiteracy. In my state, most people, even women feel they should not encourage such activities. It is not the same in urban areas. Ironically, our state is only 15% Urban. I recently returned after taking part in two important Women's Football Competitions the I-League for Women and Nationals of Women J&K. It is a very long way for females of J&K to dream for improvement. We have to work very hard and at the grassroots level.

# Kashmir FC

# Prologue

ᑭᑭᑭ

Don Bosco womens Team

In 2015, she was also awarded the title of 'Best Referee' by the All India Football Association.

Nadiya's jersey number is JJ7, the same as Ronaldo's jersey number, and is also the name of her football club where she trains under-19 girls and boys teams.

She has been associated with a homegrown football club Lone Star FC for the last two years and has been handling an important post of assistant coach for the club.

She, along with the team management has embarked on a mission to prepare the Lone Star FC to qualify for India's prestigious I-League.

Nadiya's journey into football has been no less than a fairy tale. Once a cricket freak, Nadiya landed in the world of football because of her madness of trying to kick a tennis ball every time she played cricket with the boys in her locality.

"When I was 11 years old, I had an interest in cricket. I would mostly find happiness in being a fielder rather than bowling or batting. When a ball would approach me, I would kick it with my feet, which I somehow subconsciously used to consider a football,"

Nadiya professionally started playing football in 2007, after she was noticed by an 80-year-old football Coach Mohammad Abdullah, while she was playing a random football match in her local area at Rambagh.

♡♡♡

**If football has taught me anything it is that you can overcome anything if, and only if, you love something enough**

ϸϸϸ

Having been in the spotlight for quite some time now, she inspires young girls in the Valley to get into the sport, despite all odds. Nadiya, who draws inspiration from Cristiano Ronaldo and Lionel Messi, has won 10 national and state-level awards in football and trained to be a coach with the Jammu & Kashmir Football Association (JKFA).

A product of the Government Boys High School in Natipora, Srinagar, Nadiya did not know anything apart from kicking things for fun in her childhood. "I used to kick around anything that came my way. It was part mischief, part pleasure. Till she kicked a football.

"It was big and I liked playing with it. Gradually I discovered my calling. I wanted to be a footballer" Nadiya says with a mischievous smile.

But the journey was never going to be easy. "I knew that and I was prepared for it," she says.

As a 12-year-old pushing herself to play football was a difficult choice she made. She had to endure taunts from relatives, neighbors, and even her own family members. "Everyone made fun of me. They asked why am I going around with boys. Who will like me."

Initially, even her parents did not encourage her. Coming from a not-so-economically well-off family, Nadiya had to face the brunt of even physical torture. "I was beaten with belts. My parents said sports are not for girls. I was discouraged from going out. My parents feared the taunts from neighbors and relatives," says Nadia with a hint of remorse.

**"I learned all about life with a ball at my feet"**

ᑭᑭᑭ

"My coach was very supportive. Each time someone taunted me, I told them just wait and watch."

And surely, they watched as Nadiya dribbled her way to respect on the field. Playing against boys she beat defenders, scored goals, and helped her team win.

But off the field, life continued to be bothersome. "I lost friends as parents did not allow their children to come out with me. They thought their girls will get spoilt if they see their children in my company," she says.

But Nadia was determined to change this perception.

The turning point came in 2010 when she was selected to play at the nationals. "My parents accepted me as a sportsperson. But that wasn't enough. I wanted to change the way people thought about girls my age. I wanted more girls to pursue their dreams".

She started coaching young girls. By 2015-16, she started training youngsters with the hope that she could change society's perception about girls taking up sports. The same families who never allowed their girls to go out with her now started approaching her to train their kids.

"I managed to change their mindset. I consider this an achievement," she says with a smile.

But Nadiya wasn't going to be satisfied just giving tips to change a mindset. "I wanted to prove that I can be a good coach," she says.

In 2017, both her boys' and girls' team finished on the podium in the Khelo Kashmir championship organized by the CRPF. "That brought respect."

Currently, apart from playing for clubs, she doubles up as a coach for the Kashmir Hero FC and travels through the Union Territory organizing academies to train young girls. Gradually she is making her name in a male-dominated sport.

Nadiya trains more than 40 girls and boys today. "But it's not enough I just train them. They must get a platform to showcase their talent. That is missing here in the valley," she rues.

"We need more tournaments here. There should be a proper league. The clubs should have properly structured women's teams. Local academies have girls' teams, the Kashmir Arrows too has a women's team, but this is not enough."

"The government is pushing all its resources into new talent. It needs to look at those who have given so much to the game here. Utilize our services, we can take football to the next level in the valley."

**"I want to bring change about the perception people have about Kashmir. Girls here are powerful and very bold. They are fearless. Give them the right platform, scout them and you will see them play in India colors soon."**

# Preface

“When people succeed, it is because of hard work.

In a world where athletes are treated like celebrities, we often look up to our favorite athletes for advice on and off the field. It’s inspiring to hear soccer players talk about their beloved team, their sweaty practices, and their humble successes.

1. Surpass Expectations

“There’s no better feeling than stepping out on the field and stunning them all by doing what none of them thought you could do.”

2. Overcome Hardship

"Whatever brings you down will eventually make you stronger."

3. Move On

"The past doesn't matter. Take today."

4. Appreciate Your Teammates

"It's that tingle in my stomach, that lump in my throat, and that smile on my face that tell me I am part of an incredible team."

5. Be A Role Model

"We need to have women in more powerful positions that are making decisions, so when that 10-year-old girl is looking up and wondering, 'What can I do and what do I want to be when I get older?' She has the opportunity to do and be whatever she wants."

6. It's All About Teamwork

"I have never once dribbled the whole field and scored a goal by myself."

7. Don't Take Yourself Too Seriously

"Soccer isn't brain surgery, have fun."

8. Find Intrinsic Motivation

"And then ultimately what I tell the kids is: coaches can give you information, they can give you guidelines, and they can put you in a position. But the only person who can truly make you better is you."

9. No Need to Be Feminine

"Alright, call me a tomboy. Tomboys get medals. Tomboys win championships. Tomboys can fly. Oh. And tomboys aren't boys."

10. Hard Work Will Pay Off

"I am building a fire, and every day I train, I add more fuel. At just the right moment, I light the match."

11. Legacy Matters

"Forget me. Forget my number. Forget my name. Forget I ever existed. Forget the medals won, the records broken and the sacrifices made. I want to leave a legacy where the ball keeps rolling forward, where the next generation accomplishes things so great that I am no longer remembered. So forget me, because the day I'm forgotten is the day we will succeed."

12. Improve

"I worked on my weaknesses and made them my strengths."

13. Find Self-Fulfillment

"It's about standing up and being counted and saying you're proud of who you are."

14. Live Your Passion

"Do what you love. If you love something, you aren't going to care about the sacrifices you're making to do whatever it is."

15. Be a Champion

"The vision of a champion is bent over, drenched in sweat, at the point of exhaustion when nobody else is looking."

Enjoying The Nature

# Acknowledgements

ᕈᕈᕈ

JJ7

It is no secret that many sports are male-dominated, and soccer is no exception. From as early as elementary school age, young girls are often encouraged to participate in 'feminine' sports such as netball and hockey.

Meanwhile, young boys are often encouraged to play 'masculine' sports. This leads to fewer young girls taking an interest in such sports.

Young girls who aspire to become professional soccer players also have far fewer same-sex role models to look up to. This is because female soccer is less celebrated and less televised, and therefore, there are fewer professional players.

In fact, most highly-skilled female soccer players are unable to take up the sport professionally. Less than 1% of all professional soccer players in the world are female.

This is less than female engineers (11% of the world total) and pilots (5%). Structures such as this send a damaging message to young girls- "soccer is not a viable career for women."

Despite this, the women who have managed to forge a successful soccer careers continue to inspire young girls to keep playing. We've compiled a list of quotes from soccer stars and enthusiasts, most of which are women.

"Behind all of the hours of practice, and all the coaches who pushed you, there's a little girl who first shot the ball, fell in love with the game, and never looked back..." "We decided to do this for all of the little girls across the country and around the world who deserve to have a voice, and if we don't leverage the voice we have, we are letting them down."You can't just beat a team, you have to leave a lasting impression on their minds so that they never want to see you again." "I've never scored a goal in my life without getting a pass from someone else. "Some people think soccer is a matter of life or death. I don't like that attitude. I can assure them that it is much more serious than that."

-"Being smaller than the other players just means you have to work hard to prove your strengths, toughness, and ability to compete with the bigger players."There's no better feeling than stepping out on the field and stunning them all by doing what none of them thought you could do." "Every morning, look in the mirror and tell yourself: Do not doubt my motivation, determination, toughness, commitment, perseverance, mental ability, nor my desire. Most of all, do not underestimate what I can achieve."

"Success is no accident. It is hard work, perseverance, learning, studying, sacrifice, and most of all, love of what you are doing."

"It's not about 'having time'. Everyone has the same amount of time. It is about using the time that you have."

NADIYA NIGHAT

# Courses

**COACHES ONLINE WORKSHOPS**

This is to certify that

**NADIYA NIGHAT**

from **Lonestar Kashmir Football Club**

attended the **RFYS - AIFC Coaches Online Workshops**

held on 17th, 18th & 19th May 2021.

**Siddharth Shanker**
RFYS

**Dinesh Nair**
Director - AIFC

2021 - J&K 013

Coaches Online Workshop

1:- In 2014 she qualified grassroots course.
2:- In 2015 she qualified AFC.D license.
3:- In 2016 she qualified short NIS.
4:- In 2018 she qualified AFC.C license.
5:- In 2020 she qualified IPSO scouting.

# Nationals And Pro Leagues

Sr. Women,s state level Tournament

1:- she played U-19 national in 2010.

2:- In the Year 2015 she played senior national.

3:- In the Year 2016 she played IWL ( Indian Women's league).

4:- In the Year 2018 she played senior national.

5:- In the Year 2020 she played for Karnataka League.

6:- In the Year 2021 she played senior national.

7:- In the Year 2021 she played for Kerala.
8:- In the Year 2022 she played for Karnataka.
9:- In the Year 2023 she played for Golazo Fc in Pune.

# Working Places As A Coach

1:- In the Year 2018, she worked as a head coach in Mumbai FLA.

2:-In the Year 2019, she worked as a head coach at Haryana Alakpura FC.

3:- In the Year 2020, she worked as an Assistant Coach at Lonestar Kashmir FC in the 2nd Division I league.

4:- In the Year 2021, worked for Real Kashmir FC as a Head Coach of the Women's Team.

5:- In the Year 2021, she worked with Lone Star Kashmir FC as an Assistant Coach.

6:- In the year 2021, she worked with Golaza FC as a Head Coach.

7:- In the Year 2022, she worked as a Head Coach of Golaza FC in Pune.

8:- In the Year 2023, she is working with the same Club in Pune. They start Residential Academy for boys and girls.

Womens football Traning Camp 2022

ÞÞÞ

# Achievements

She is the first female football coach of Kashmir and started her journey in 2007. Her hard work, Achievements, and success made her popular day by day. Nadiya, now, has received 10 national and state-level awards. She runs a football academy in Rambagh and trains more than 30 children, including girls.

AWARD

*This Award is Presented By*

Global Human Rights Trust

SPECIAL STATUS : UNITED NATION DEPTT. OF ECONOMIC AND SOCIAL AFFAIR

*Presented To*

Nadiya Nighat

Srinagar J&K

SPORTS WOMEN OF THE YEAR

*The Human Rights Nobel Award is the highest Honorary Award of the Republic of India. instituted on 3rd of January 2021. The Award is conferred in recognition of exceptional service, performance of the highest order, without distinction of Caste, Color, Creed, Religion and Sex.*

Dr. H R Rehman
(Managing Director)
HRNA

Human Rights Nobel Award ($3^{rd}$ Jan 2021)

INTERNATIONAL
PROFESSIONAL
SCOUTING
ORGANISATION

# AIFF / IPSO CERTIFICATE

IPSO is pleased to confirm that

Nadiya Nighat

has successfully passed the test of **LEVEL I COURSE**
in **FOOTBALL SCOUTING**
and qualified for the **IPSO Membership**

Membership No. 2677

Mr. Colin Chambers

ymca awards

Mr. Kamil Potrykus

IPSO

Certificate of
ACHIEVEMENT
PRESENTED TO
NADIA NIGHAT
International Women's Day Celebration

#2018

#Assistant Coach

#U-12 girls football Tournament 2018

GOVERNMENT OF JAMMU & KASHMIR

Regd. No. 0019

DIRECTORATE GENERAL OF YOUTH SERVICES & SPORTS

56th NATIONAL SCHOOL GAMES

(Under Aegis of S.G.F.I.)

Certificate

Participation Certificate

Name: Nadiya

Parentage: Mohd Sidiq Batloo

Date of Birth: 11-11-1996.

Age Group: Under 19 (Girls)

State/U.T.: J&K

Game: FOOTBALL

Date: 27-09-2010 to 01-10-2010

Venue: JAMMU (Tawi)

G. M. Dar
Director
Youth Services & Sports
J&K Govt.

S.A Lahaswal
Director General
Youth Services & Sports
J&K Govt.

56th School National Games

9 798889 592624

Printed by Libri Plureos GmbH in Hamburg,
Germany